GUINNESS WORLD RECORDS

TOP 10

Bizarre Bug Records

Compiled by Celeste Lee and Ryan Herndon

For Guinness World Records:
Laura Plunkett, Craig Glenday, Stuart Claxton

SCHOLASTIC INC.
New York Toronto London Auckland Sydney
Mexico City New Delhi Hong Kong Buenos Aires

P9-DHC-411

The publisher would like to thank the following for
their kind permission to use their photographs in this book:

Cover, title page Jungle Nymph © Tom Kidd/REX USA; 1 Locusts © Ng Han Guan/AP Wide World Photos;
2 Arthropod © Steve Reekie; 3 Girl with Caterpillar © Arthur Tilley/Taxi/Getty Images; 4 (top) Burmese
Mantid © Shutterstock, (bottom) Treehopper © Dr. Paul A. Zahl/Photo Researchers, Inc.; 5 Stick Insect
© Ted Kinsman/Photo Researchers, Inc.; 6 Mayfly © Larry Katz/AnimalsAnimals-Earth Scenes;
7 Monarch Butterfly © Luis C. Tejo/Morguefile.com; 9 Rolling Caterpillar © Dr. John Brackenbury/Photo
Researchers, Inc.; 10 Child with Butterfly © Erin Hogan/Photodisc/Getty Images; 11 Dragonfly © Robert
Lubeck/AnimalsAnimals-Earth Scenes; 12 Swallowtail Butterfly © Roger Wilmshurst/FLPA; 13 Australian
Dragonfly courtesy of Sara Halas; 14 Dragonfly Eyes © Ifa-Bilderteam Gmbh/Oxford Scientific; 15 Robot
and Bug © Louie Psihoyos/CORBIS; 16 Boy with Beetle © Mitsuhiko Imamori/Minden Pictures;
17 Cricket on Tongue © Richard Drew/AP Wide World Photos; 18 Splendor Beetle © Natural History
Museum London; 19 Click Beetle © Larry F. Jernigan/Jupiter Images; 20 Stag Beetle © Creatas/Jupiter
Images; 21 (top) Goliath Beetle © Stockbyte/Jupiter Images, (bottom) Rhinoceros Beetle © Wolfgang
Kaehler/CORBIS; 22 Bee Swarm © Philip Bailey/CORBIS; 23 Argentine Ant © George D. Lepp/CORBIS;
24 Ants Moving Rice Grain © Pascal Goetgheluck/Photo Researchers, Inc.; 25 Ant Supercolony Map
courtesy of Laurent Keller; 26 Wasp © Kim Taylor/Bruce Coleman Inc.; 27 Wasp Nest courtesy of Guinness
World Records; 28 (top) African Honeybee © Scott Camazine/Photo Researchers, Inc., (bottom) Beehive
© Ken Thomas/Photo Researchers, Inc.; 29 Ladybug Flying © A. Syred/Photo Researchers, Inc.;
30 Stag Beetle © Toshiyuki Aizawa/Reuters.

Guinness World Records Limited has a very thorough accreditation system
for records verification. However, while every effort is made to ensure accuracy,
Guinness World Records Limited cannot be held responsible for any
errors contained in this work. Feedback from our readers on
any point of accuracy is always welcomed.

© 2006 Guinness World Records Limited, a HIT Entertainment Limited Company

No part of this work may be reproduced, stored in a retrieval system, or transmitted
in any form or by any means, electronic, mechanical, photocopying, recording,
or otherwise without written permission of the publisher. For information regarding
permission, write to Scholastic Inc., Attention: Permissions Department,
557 Broadway, New York, NY 10012.

Published by Scholastic Inc. SCHOLASTIC and associated logos are trademarks
and/or registered trademarks of Scholastic Inc.

ISBN 0-439-87416-5

Designed by Michelle Martinez Design, Inc.
Photo Research by Els Rijper
Records from the Archives of Guinness World Records

20 19 18 17   40   14/0

Printed in the U.S.A.

First printing, November 2006

Visit Guinness World Records at www.guinnessworldrecords.com

Do bugs really "rule" the world?
If you scooped up all the bugs in the world, they would
weigh more than every person and animal combined!

This *Guinness World Records*™ book explores 10 buggy
record-holders. You'll discover there's more
to a bug's life than meets the eye!

THE EGG HATCHES

Scientists use another name for bugs: *hexapoda*, or six-legged *arthropod*. An arthropod is an animal whose skeleton is on the outside of its body. This outer skeleton is called an *exoskeleton*.

True bugs have six legs, two antennae, and three body sections — a head (front), thorax (middle), and abdomen (end). Each bug has its own scientific name and is in a special grouping called a *species*. There are more than *five million* bug species!

ABDOMEN

HEAD

THORAX

Spiders or arachnids are arthropods, but have 8 legs!

A bug's life is lived in three main stages. Mother bugs lay thousands of **eggs**. An egg hatches into a **larva**. The larva grows up to become an **adult**.

This process is called **metamorphosis**. Each stage of development causes a change to the insect's body. Maggots grow up to be flies. Caterpillars become butterflies or moths.

Some bugs have four life stages. Look for the *pupal* stage on page 8.

Bugs use lots of tricks to get out of trouble. Some fly, swim, dig, or roll away. Many hide right under our noses! Insects, animals, and sometimes people hide from enemies by matching the colors of their scales, fur, or clothing to their environment. This trick is called **camouflage**.

Birds fly past a Burmese mantid camouflaged as a "pretty flower" (above). Treehoppers look like a plant's thorns, and their spiny shells are just as tough (left). So take a closer look, because that tree twig or leaf might really be a live bug!

Largest Insect Egg

There are about 2,000 different species of stick insect. Camouflage is their only defense against hungry birds. When these bugs stand still, they look like brown or green sticks, twigs, or leaves (below).

In Malaysia, one species *(Heteropteryx dilitata)* is 6 inches tall, and its eggs are the largest in the bug kingdom. Each egg is 0.5 inches long — about the size of a peanut! Other bugs and animals like to eat these eggs. For protection, these eggs are camouflaged to look like plant seeds.

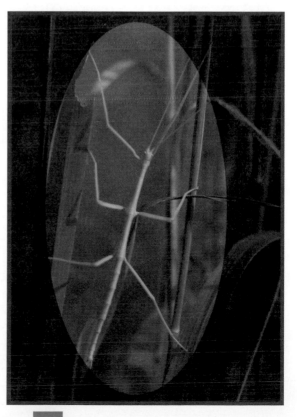

Shortest-Lived Insect

Mayflies spend most of their lives getting ready to be a grown-up. The mayfly egg hatches into a larva, known as a **naiad**. Because the naiad lives underwater, a gill-like organ lets this bug breathe like a fish!

For up to three years, the naiad grows larger by **molting**, or shedding its exoskeleton. After its last molt, the mayfly's wings come out and it becomes an adult (left).

The adult can fly, but it doesn't have a mouth or stomach. This is why adult mayflies live only between one hour and two days. The adult mayfly's job is to find a mate, lay eggs, then die. A new mayfly hatches and the entire life cycle begins again.

The mayfly swims or flies away from danger. Other bugs scare off animals by pretending to be dangerous. When the tephritid fly flaps its wings, it looks like a jumping spider. The owl butterfly opens its colorful wings, and predators believe an owl's face is staring at them!

Another bug trick is eating poisonous plants. The monarch butterfly (below) and red milkweed beetle don't get sick eating milkweed. But if a bird eats these bugs, it throws up and learns not to eat these kinds of nasty-tasting bugs again.

A butterfly or moth hatches from an egg and begins metamorphosis as a caterpillar (see chart). A caterpillar eats a lot because it **molts** or grows in size 30,000 times between the **larval** and **pupal stages**. The caterpillar sleeps inside a cocoon and wakes up as an adult butterfly or moth. Then it flies away to lay more eggs.

Humans don't molt. Our bones grow inside our bodies.

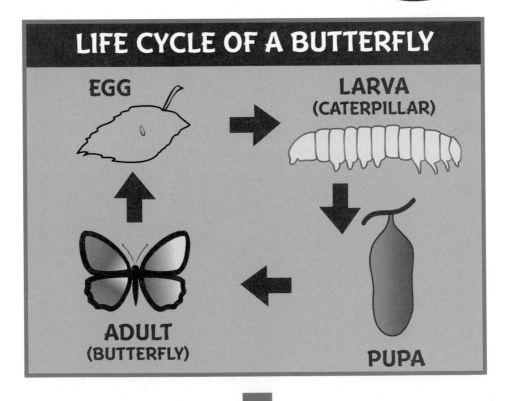

LIFE CYCLE OF A BUTTERFLY

EGG

LARVA (CATERPILLAR)

ADULT (BUTTERFLY)

PUPA

Fastest Caterpillar

A mother-of-pearl moth was once a speedy caterpillar (*Pleuroptya ruralis*). When scared, this caterpillar curls up into a ball and rolls away at 15 inches per second (below). It is the only land insect to escape in this way. This caterpillar's speed is equal to a car's speed of 150 miles per hour — faster than any car should drive on a highway!

The word *caterpillar* means "hairy cat"!

FLY AWAY

Do you wonder how a butterfly can land on your fingertip? Or why a fly can take off from the edge of your potato chip before you catch it? Incredible eyes and amazing wings have helped insects survive for more than 300 million years.

Insects developed wings to become the first flying creatures *before* birds. Wings are handy to have in finding food, escaping from enemies, and meeting mates. Some bugs even use their wings to fly in search of warmer weather.

An insect's exoskeleton is incredibly light, yet it keeps the bug's body temperature just right. Having an exoskeleton is like wearing an all-weather raincoat. A bug can fly in any kind of weather.

Bzz, bzz! Insects stay in the air by flapping their wings super fast in a figure-eight shape. Bees beat their wings 100 times per second. Tiny mosquito wings vibrate *1,000* times per second.

However, certain tropical butterflies can fly faster than 20 miles per hour. But the number of actual wing beats per second is slow. Most butterflies flutter their pair of beautiful wings at only 8 to 12 times per second. The swallowtail butterfly takes its time. Its wings beat only 5 beats per *second*, that is 300 times per minute — slower than any other insect.

Fastest Flying Insect

Does a dragonfly look like a dragon? We don't know why the bug got its name, but fossils show that ancient dragonflies were huge. One fossil measured 2 feet wide! Today's species are smaller, but still impressive in size and speed.

A bug lives longer if it can fly faster than the bird chasing it. One species of Australian dragonfly *(Austrophlebia costalis)* zips along at 36 miles per hour (below). That's as fast as a lion can run!

Dragonflies are sharp-eyed hunters. Each eye has 30,000 lenses with 360-degree vision (below).

This means they can spot a buggy meal in every direction. As an underwater larva, a dragonfly grabs meals such as tadpoles, small fish, and other insect larvae by shooting out a spear from its lower jaw. As an adult, it uses its long, spindly legs to catch food in midair flight. Now *that's* fast food!

Going Buggy

Sometimes nature gives engineers and scientists new ideas for inventions.

For example, many insects hover, or float in the same spot by rapidly beating their wings. Inspired by such movements, engineers built machines, such as the helicopter, to use the same flying ability. Scientists are building bug-sized, flying robots to explore outer space and other places too dangerous for people to go, such as earthquake or flood-disaster areas.

BEETLE-MANIA

Fossils of beetles date back 250 million years. Scientists estimate that more than 350,000 different species of beetles live in the world today — more than any other creature!

Many beetle species are helpful to us. Dung beetles feed on the waste of large animals. Burying beetles eat decaying animal bodies. These beetles keep our environment clean. But some beetles are harmful and eat our crops and the wood used in our homes.

People around the world also eat beetles and other insects (below). Bugs are filled with protein and vitamins. In Thailand, people eat deep-fried grasshoppers and beetles. In Africa, caterpillars are considered a treat. In Ecuador, ants are fried or — *gulp* — eaten alive!

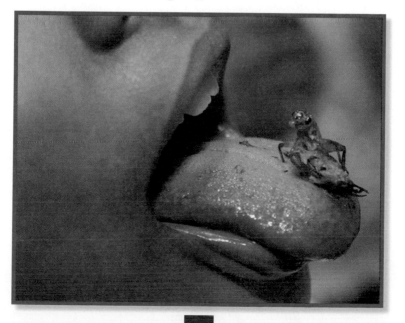

Oldest Insect

Ancient Egyptians treasured beetles as a symbol of rebirth. Some bugs may live for only a few hours. But splendor beetles *(Buprestis aurulenta)* don't need to be reborn so often, because this species can make a larval stage last 20 to 50 *years*.

One amazing specimen was found in Essex, England. On May 27, 1983, this splendor beetle (below) crawled out from beneath a house's wooden staircase and into the record books. It had been living for about 47 years as a larva!

Highest G-Force Endured by an Insect

A noisy hinge on the body of the click beetle *(Athous haemorrhoidalis)* saves its life. If the beetle lands on its back, it snaps its hinge to flip over. If a predator grabs the beetle, the hinge's "click" is an alarm set off to scare others.

The click beetle makes its escape — and sets a record — by snapping its body into the shape of an upside-down letter *V*. Then it shoots upward 11.8 inches into the air. The gravitational force (G-Force) against its body is 400 G — more than any other insect can survive! People normally experience 1 G of gravity pulling our bodies toward the ground.

Most Expensive Insect

Some people, such as butterfly collectors, beekeepers, and anthill farmers, work and live with bugs.

In Japan, pet bugs are more popular than cats or dogs. One 1.25-inch-long beetle costs $20. But one stag beetle (*Dorcus hopei*) at 3.10 inches long cost a Japanese collector more than 10 million yen in 1999 (below). That price tag was equal to $90,000 — the price of a small house in Japan!

Heavy Lifters

Pet beetles that also tip the record-setting scales are goliath and rhinoceros beetles (*Scarabaeidae*). A live goliath beetle (above) weighed about 3.5 ounces — heavier than a large chocolate bar. This earned it the Guinness World Record for **Heaviest Insect**.

Heaviest doesn't always mean strongest. Can you believe that a bug is stronger than an elephant? To compare, an elephant would have to carry 851 other elephants to *proportionally* beat the strength of the rhinoceros beetle (below). In real life, an elephant can't lift even one elephant on its back. A rhinoceros beetle can lift 850 times its own weight, making it the **Strongest Insect**.

ALL HAIL THE QUEEN

Bugs use camouflage to hide or wings to fly away. They also know that safety lies in large numbers. One bee can't protect its honey from a bear. But 100 bees are big trouble for that bear.

Have you ever found an anthill or beehive? These are the homes of *social insects*. These bugs work and live together in a *colony*, just like people live together in a town. Some examples of social insects are ants, bees, termites, and wasps.

People can choose what job they want to do. But social insects are born *into* a job. **Workers** build the nest and carry food into the hive. **Soldiers** protect the home. Others care for the eggs and raise larvae (below). There are even bugs who must take the trash out!

The most important bug is the **queen**. She lays the eggs and rules over the group. Every bug knows it must do its job or the community will fail.

Bug colonies have many rooms — even bathrooms!

Ants have two stomachs. One stomach stores the ant's food. The second stomach, called the **crop**, stores food to share with the colony.

Ants "talk" by touching antennae and can tell if the other ant is a friend or an enemy. One ant can carry an object several times heavier than itself. But teams of ants have been seen carrying objects up to 50 times heavier than one ant (below).

Largest Colony of Ants

Scientists found a supersized ant colony is taking over Europe. A species of Argentine ant *(Linepithema humile)* has tunneled through four countries: Italy, France, Spain, and Portugal (see map). This ant colony is 3,700 miles long — wider than the USA!

These millions of queens and billions of ants recognize one another, even if one ant comes from France and another from Spain. They kill other bugs from outside the colony. Scientists are studying the colony to make sure these ants really don't take over the whole world!

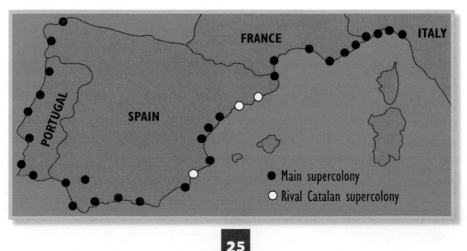

PORTUGAL

SPAIN

FRANCE

ITALY

● Main supercolony
○ Rival Catalan supercolony

Wasps build large, round nests that hang from tree branches or are stuck to people's houses. Tell a grown-up if you see a nest, but stay away from it! Wasps protect their homes by stinging anybody who gets too close to the nest.

A wasp nest is made of wood pulp. Wasps pluck wood from fences, telephone poles, and even cardboard. They fly back to where they want to build a nest and start chewing. Wood fiber mixed with wasp spit makes a paste that the wasps use to build their nest.

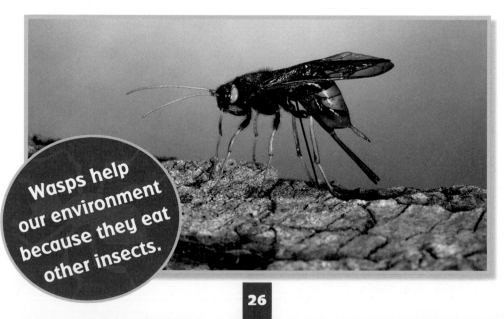

Wasps help our environment because they eat other insects.

Largest Wasp Nest

In the United States, wasps move out of a nest in the fall and build another nest in the springtime. But in tropical countries, a wasp colony can keep growing and growing.

A man named Yoichiro Kawamura found an empty wasp nest in Yonegaoka, Japan (right). The nest was measured on May 18, 1999. Its size and weight set a new Guinness World Record. The nest was 8 feet around and weighed 17 pounds 8 ounces!

Yummy Honey

Bees may sting, but they also make the world taste and smell better. These bugs land on a flower to drink its nectar (above). The flower's pollen sticks to the bee. The bee visits another flower, and the pollen is moved between the plants. This is how bees *pollinate* 80 percent of the world's crops.

Bees fly back to their home, called a *hive* (below). Inside, the bees use nectar in making a sweet treat: honey! This was the first type of sugar enjoyed by people. Stone Age cave paintings in Spain show a human getting honey from beehives. Honey is used around the world to make candy and to sweeten food and medicine.

Nectar from more than a million flowers makes just one jar of honey!

We can't live without bugs. Bees pollinate flowers, fruits, and crops. Ants and beetles keep the soil healthy. Animals, and some humans, need bugs for their diet.

Bugs take care of the world and share it with us. Shouldn't we do a better job of sharing the world with some of them?

If a ladybug gets lost in your house, don't squash it. Scoop it up, go outside, and let that ladybug fly away home (below). After all, it is said to be good luck!

Every day, scientists learn more
about how tiny bugs make big changes in our world.

Guinness World Records keeps track of these
discoveries to tell you about the largest, fastest, strongest,
and most bizarre bugs of all!

Attempting to break records or set new records can be dangerous.
Appropriate advice should be taken first, and all record attempts
are undertaken entirely at the participant's risk. In no circumstances
will Guinness World Records Limited or Scholastic Inc. have any
liability for death or injury suffered in any record attempts.
Guinness World Records Limited has complete discretion over
whether or not to include any particular records
in the annual *Guinness World Records* book.